THE NEWEST NINJA CREAM

Layla F. Kennel

Contents

1. Introduction — 1

2. Chapter 2 — 15

3. Chapter 3 — 21

4. Chapter 4 — 24

5. Chapter 5 — 27

6. Chapter 6 — 29

7. Chapter 7 — 31

8. Chapter 8 — 33

9. Chapter 9 — 35

10. Chapter 10 — 37

11. Chapter 11 — 40

12. Chapter 12 — 42

13. Chapter 13 — 44

14. Chapter 14 — 46

15. Chapter 15   48

16. Chapter 16   50

17. Chapter 17   52

18. Chapter 18   54

19. Chapter 19   56

20. Chapter 20   58

21. Chapter 21   60

22. Chapter 22   62

23. Chapter 23   64

24. Chapter 24   66

25. Chapter 25   68

26. Chapter 26   71

27. Chapter 27   74

28. Chapter 28   77

29. Chapter 29   80

30. Chapter 30   84

31. Chapter 31   88

32. Chapter 32   93

33. Chapter 33   97

34. Chapter 34 100

35. Chapter 35 104

36. Chapter 36 108

37. Chapter 37 112

38. Chapter 38 115

39. Chapter 39 118

40. Chapter 40 121

41. Chapter 41 124

42. Chapter 42 127

43. Chapter 43 130

44. Chapter 44 134

45. Chapter 45 138

46. Chapter 46 142

47. Chapter 47 146

48. Chapter 48 150

49. Chapter 49 154

50. Chapter 50 158

51. Chapter 51 160

52. Chapter 52 162

53. Chapter 53	164
54. Chapter 54	167
55. Chapter 55	169
56. Chapter 56	172
57. Chapter 57	175
58. Chapter 58	178
59. Chapter 59	183
60. Chapter 60	186
61. Chapter 61	189
62. Chapter 62	192
63. Chapter 63	195
64. Chapter 64	198
65. Chapter 65	201
66. Chapter 66	204
67. Chapter 67	205
68. Chapter 68	209
69. Chapter 69	213
70. Chapter 70	220

Chapter One

Introduction

Who doesn't like ice cream? Ice cream is undeniably one of the world's most popular frozen desserts. It's difficult to resist its sweet flavor, creamy texture, and refreshing coolness, as anyone can attest!

You may be surprised to learn that you can now start making your own ice cream at home. You can make your own ice cream at any time with Ninja Creami. You can also make smoothies, gelatos, sorbets, and milkshakes.

2 THE NEWEST NINJA CREAM

Don't make the mistake of assuming that the machine is costly or difficult to use. This is not true. This is one home appliance that is not only affordable but also a good investment. And, once you've read the instructions for operating, maintaining, and caring for it, you'll see that it's very simple to use.

It's not surprising, given that it comes from one of the world's leading kitchen appliance manufacturers. Ninja Kitchen has become well-known for producing a wide range of efficient and innovative kitchen appliances, including pressure cookers, air fryers, blenders, and many more.

What are you waiting for? You can easily prepare delicious frozen desserts for yourself and your family using the Ninja Creami.

What is Ninja Creami?

Introducing the Ninja CREAMi, a cutting-edge new home ice cream maker that enables you to instantly convert frozen bases into ice cream, milkshakes, sorbets, and other frozen desserts. It would take hours to turn a uniformly frozen block into an extraordinarily smooth and creamy texture with other techniques, but thanks to the Ninja CREAMi's patented technology, it only takes minutes. "Creamify" is the name of this process. You have the option of using your base right away or freezing it for later use after it has undergone this metamorphosis.

Buttons & User Guide

- Install Light: If the device is incorrectly assembled, the install light will not turn on. If it blinks, make sure the bowl is inserted properly. Check to see if the paddle is in the right spot and if the light is solid.

- Progress Bar: The total progress of the currently utilized One-Touch Program is shown by the progress bar. All four progress bar LEDs will blink twice when the task is finished, after which they will all go dark.

- One-Touch Programs: The device's pre-set functions run for 1 to 2 12 minutes, creating incredible meals quickly. However, based on the recipe and the ingredients, the preparation time may vary.

Let's take a look at some of the Ninja CREAMi's special features and benefits.

• Quick Processing Time: To produce the creamiest, smoothest ice cream, sorbet, and gelato, the machine chums the ice cream mixture.

• Simple to Create Multiple Flavors: Start with a simple vanilla foundation and enjoy making two, three, or even six different flavors.

• Make-Ahead Feature: You can prepare as many different flavors of ice cream in advance and store them in the freezer for when you're ready to consume the CREAMi and process the base.

• Easy to Clean: Except for the part with the Dual Drive Motor, the Ninja CREAMi is dishwasher safe on the top rack. If you don't have a dishwasher, simply use warm water and soap to clean the parts.

• Smaller Batch Size: You won't need to keep a large ice cream container in your freezer because of the reduced batch size. Simply purchase additional pint containers and have an ice cream social or tasting party with as many different flavors as you'd like!

• Ice Cream, Sorbet, and Light Ice Cream Modes: Ice cream, gelato (Italian ice cream), sorbet (fruit or vegetable juice that has been frozen and treated), and light ice cream may all be made at the touch of a button. Greater processing time at faster speeds is necessary to break up ice crystals and produce creamy sorbets and smoothie bowls,. No matter what you want to prepare, the machine takes care of everything for you, so you don't have to do any guesswork. How to Clean & Maintain Ninja CREAMi

Cleaning

⬚ Hand-Washing: Wash the containers, lids, and paddle in warm, soapy water. Use a cleaning tool with a handle for dishes to completely clean the paddle. Thoroughly rinse and air-dry each component.

☐ Dishwasher: The device includes lids, dishwasher-safe containers, and a paddle (top rack only). Put the paddle, pint, outer bowl, and lids in the dishwasher after making sure they are all separated.

☐ Outer Bowl Lid: Ingredients may get stuck under the paddle, therefore take out the paddle before cleaning the outside bowl cover. Fill up the drain holes on either side of the paddle release lever with warm water. Place the lid in this position: lever side down, to completely drain it. Remove the center lip seal of the outer bowl cover, which is made of a dark grey rubber material. After that, the lid can be manually cleaned with warm, soapy water or put in the dishwasher.

⫿ Motor Base: Unplug the motor base before cleaning it, and then wipe it off with some water. Avoid using abrasive cloths, pads, or brushes to clean the base. Use a moist cloth to wipe down the spindle underneath the control panel after each use. To remove any liquid that got stuck between the motor base and the platform, raise the platform. The handle of the outer bowl should be positioned in the center below the control panel and on the motor base. By turning the handle to the right, you can raise the platform. Then use a moist towel to clean the area between the base and elevated platform.

Storing

To store the cord, wrap it around the hook-and-loop fastener at the back of the motor base. Do not wrap the cable around the base's bottom for storage. Any remaining attachments should be kept near the device or in a cabinet where they will not be destroyed or become a hazard.

Resetting the Motor

This device features a one-of-a-kind safety mechanism that protects the motor and the system if it is accidentally overloaded.

If the unit is overloaded, the motor will be temporarily disabled. If this occurs, follow the instructions below to reset the device:

- Unplug the device from the power supply.
- Allow the device to cool for 15 minutes.

• Remove the outer bowl cover and the paddle. Make sure the lid assembly is free of debris.

The Ninja CREAMi is a cutting-edge kitchen appliance that quickly produces delicious ice creams, smoothies, sorbets, milkshakes, and other desserts. Almost all your sweet tooth cravings are covered by the device's extensive list of pre-set settings. The gadget is incredibly practical and simple to use. It's additionally easy to keep and clean. Dishwasher safety applies to the paddle, lid, and containers. But never submerge the motor base in liquids when cleaning it; simply use a moist cloth. The Ninja CREAMi is an ice cream lover's dream come true. With the aid of this cookbook, we hope you enjoy creating (and eating!) delectable recipes.

Main Functions of the Ninja CREAMi

The Ninja CREAMi can make the following delectable frozen treats:

▯ ICE CREAM

This feature creates classic recipes for indulgence. It turns dairy and dairy substitutes into scoopable, creamy, and thick ice creams.

▯ LITE ICE CREAM

This function should be used if you care about your health and want an ice cream substitute that is low in fat or sugar. Recipes for both the keto and paleo diets work well with it.

▯ GELATO

This function can be used with custard bases for ice creams, such as Italian style. It yields decadent and delectable desserts.

12 THE NEWEST NINJA CREAM

☐ SORBET

You can use this function to make delectable creamy delights with high sugar and water content, primarily fruit-based recipes.

☐ MILKSHAKE

This option is for you if you want a quick and thick milkshake. Simply add milk, ice cream, and your preferred mix-ins. Your delicious milkshake will be ready in only a few moments,.

☐ SMOOTHIE BOWL

This feature is appropriate for you if your recipe calls for fresh or frozen fruits or vegetables. Simply combine juice, dairy, or dairy substitutes with the vegetables or fruits, and you're ready to go!

☐ MIX-IN

To personalize a freshly processed foundation or store-bought treat, you can stir in frozen fruits, bits of nuts, cookies, cereal, or candies. Mix-ins should be introduced in the middle of the CREA-Mi Pint, per recommendation. After the pint has been processed, use a spoon to make a hole that is 112 inches broad and extends to the bottom. Add the chopped or broken mix-ins to the hole after that, and then use this function to process the mixture.

⬚ RE-SPIN

You can use this function to achieve a more refined and smooth texture after using any of the pre-set functions. We recommend using this function when the base temperature is less than -7°F and the overall texture of the recipe is crumbly rather than creamy.

Tips

- We do not recommend using the RE-SPIN function before the MIX-IN pre-set program.

- To end any of the pre-set functions, simply press the illuminated function button.

Chapter Two

Vanilla

Vanilla is America's preferred ice cream flavor above all others for a reason: it's straightforward and works with everything. Cary Frye, an expert in ice cream and vice president of IDFA, adds, "Because it is creamy and delicious and because it complements so many other desserts and delights, vanilla has long been the most popular ice cream flavor. It tastes fantastic on top of a warm slice of apple pie, a sundae with whipped cream and fudge sauce, a root beer float, or any other frozen treat." (Source: WISTV. This flavor is very widely available at your local grocery store!)

Chocolate

Like vanilla, chocolate is popular because of its versatility. It comes in a wide variety, unlike vanilla, including chocolate chunk, fudge swirl, and mudslide. Additionally, many people like chocolate ice cream since it may be either rich or light. It can either be consumed on its own or as part of a sundae.

Cookies & Cream

Cookies & cream is a new twist on vanilla because it contains cookie pieces, allowing your customers to consume a lot without becoming tired of their ice cream. This ice cream works well in ice cream sandwiches and waffle cones, too. With the help of this mix and shaper, try making your own!

Mint Chocolate Chip

This minty ice cream is popular because it is unlike any other ice cream. It's light and refreshing, with sweet chocolate chunks. The flavors are balanced so that it is neither too rich nor too tart.

Chocolate Chip Cookie Dough

This is yet another interesting variation on vanilla ice cream. It combines cookies, America's favorite warm treat, and vanilla, America's favorite ice cream. It combines two desserts that your customers already enjoy. Serve it in these amusing cow cups!

Buttered Pecan

For good reason, buttered pecan is a classic Southern treat! The ideal indulgent treat, in my opinion. The crispy pecan chunks and silky ice cream are the ideal complements to one another. Because there is just enough saltiness to balance out the sweetness, this is a popular favorite.

Birthday Cake

Many people enjoy this, not just on their birthdays. Sprinkles, cake pieces, and thick buttercream frosting are all included. Additionally, the vibrant icing and sprinkles make it a success right away! Try eating it with these colorful spoons to make it more fun!

Strawberry

This traditional fruit-based ice cream flavor tastes fantastic both on its own and in a banana split. It has strawberry bits and is sweet and creamy. Any treat would be excellent with this ice cream! Use these vibrant milkshake straws when blending them into a milkshake!

Moose tracks

This tasty treat includes lots of pieces! It consists of fudge, peanut butter cups, and vanilla ice cream. It offers a fresh perspective on vanilla ice cream. Enough is going on for it to be great on its own without needing to be a sundae.

Neapolitan

20 THE NEWEST NINJA CREAM

Finally, this is vanilla, chocolate, and strawberry ice cream. It's the perfect combination of three delicious things. Because each scoop of this frozen treat could have all three flavors, it would be great in a banana split! Try elevating your favorite treat with these banana split containers.

Chapter Three

Fruit Carrot Ice Cream

Prep time: 5 minutes | Cook time: 5 minutes| Serves 4

¾ cup heavy cream

½ cup milk

⅓ cup orange juice

¾ cup sugar

¼ cup frozen carrots

¼ cup pineapple chunks

1. In a bowl, add the heavy cream, milk, orange juice and sugar and beat until sugar is dissolved.

2. In an empty Ninja CREAMi pint container, place the carrots and pineapple chunks and top with milk mixture.

3. Cover the container with storage lid and freeze for 24 hours.

4. After 24 hours, remove the lid from container and arrange into the Outer Bowl of Ninja CREAMi.

5. Install the Creamerizer Paddle onto the lid of Outer Bowl.

6. Then rotate the lid clockwise to lock.

7. Press Power button to turn on the unit.

8. Then press Ice Cream button.

9. When the program is completed, turn the Outer Bowl and release it from the machine.

10. Select the Re-spin function if, after processing, you want your processed treat softer and creamier.

11. Transfer the ice cream into serving bowls and serve immediately.

Chapter Four

Chia Seed Ice Cream

Prep time: 5 minutes | Cook time: 5 minutes| Serves 4

¼ cup milk

2 tablespoons honey

½ cup vanilla whole milk Greek yogurt

2 tablespoons chia seeds

1. Mix all the ingredients and beat until smooth.

2. Transfer the mixture into an empty Ninja CREAMi Pint.

3. Cover the pint with the lid and freeze for 24 hours.

4. After 24 hours, remove the lid and place the pint into the outer bowl of the Ninja CREAMi.

5. Install the Creamerizer Paddle onto the lid of the outer bowl, then rotate the lid clockwise to lock.

6. Turn the unit on.

7. Press the ICE CREAM button.

8. When the program is complete, turn the outer bowl and release it from the unit.

9.

Select the Re-spin function if, after processing, you want your processed treat softer and creamier.

10. Serve in bowls.

Chapter Five

Vanilla Ice Cream

Prep time: 5 minutes | Cook time: 5 minutes| Serves 5

6 frozen bananas, peeled

1/4 cup ultra-filtered 2% milk

1/2 cup Greek yogurt

1 tablespoon honey

1/4 teaspoon pure vanilla extract

1/2 teaspoon pink Himalayan salt, crushed

1. Add all the ingredients to a large mixing bowl.

2. Transfer to the Ninja Creami pint container.

3. Mix until smooth.

4. Select the Re-spin function if, after processing, you want your processed treat softer and creamier.

5. Spoon into individual bowls and freeze leftovers in an airtight container.

Chapter Six

Bourbon Ice Cream

Prep time: 10 minutes | Cook time: 5 minutes| Serves 5

6 frozen bananas, peeled

1 cup Greek yogurt

1 teaspoon pure vanilla extract

1/4 cup brown sugar substitute

3 tablespoons bourbon

1. Add all the ingredients to a large mixing bowl.

2. Transfer to the Ninja Creami pint container.

3. Mix until smooth.

4. Select the Re-spin function if, after processing, you want your processed treat softer and creamier.

5. Spoon into individual bowls and freeze leftovers in an airtight container.

Chapter Seven

Coconut Caramel Ice Cream

Prep time: 5 minutes | Cook time: 5 minutes| Serves 4

6 frozen bananas, peeled

1 bag fresh frozen coconut

1 teaspoon pure coconut extract

1 teaspoon brown sugar substitute

2 teaspoons pure vanilla extract

1/4 cup calorie free caramel sauce

1. Add all the ingredients to a large mixing bowl.

2. Transfer to the Ninja Creami pint container.

3. Mix until smooth.

4. Select the Re-spin function if, after processing, you want your processed treat softer and creamier.

5. Spoon into individual bowls and freeze leftovers in an airtight container.

6. Top with caramel sauce.

7. Freeze leftovers in an airtight container.

Chapter Eight

Mint Chocolate Chip Ice Cream

Prep time: 5 minutes | Cook time: 5 minutes|
Serves 3

9 frozen bananas, peeled

1/2 frozen avocado, peeled and pitted

1 tablespoon honey

5 mint leaves, chopped

1/2 teaspoon mint extract

1/3 cup 85% dark cacao bar, chopped

1. Add all the ingredients to a large mixing bowl.

2. Transfer to the Ninja Creami pint container.

3. Mix until smooth.

4. Select the Re-spin function if, after processing, you want your processed treat softer and creamier.

5. Spoon into individual bowls and freeze leftovers in an airtight container.

Chapter Nine

Peanut Butter Pretzel Ice Cream

Prep time: 5 minutes | Cook time: 5 minutes| Serves 4

12 frozen bananas, peeled

3 tablespoons all-natural peanut butter, no sugar added

1 teaspoon honey

1/4 teaspoon pure vanilla extract, frozen

1 tablespoon ultra-filtered milk or almond milk, frozen

1/2 cup gluten-free pretzels, roughly chopped

1. Add bananas, butter, honey, vanilla extract and milk to a large mixing bowl.

2. Transfer to the Ninja Creami pint container.

3. Mix until smooth.

4. Select the Re-spin function if, after processing, you want your processed treat softer and creamier.

5. Scoop ice cream into waffle cones and top with pretzel pieces.

6. Freeze leftover soft-serve in an airtight container.

Chapter Ten

Chocolate Ice Cream

Prep time: 2 hours 5 minutes | Cook time: 15 minutes| Serves 4

12 frozen bananas, peeled

2 cups Greek yogurt, vanilla flavored

1/2 cup unsweetened cocoa

1/2 cup coffee

3 tablespoons Neufchatel or cream cheese substitute

2 tablespoons honey

1/3 cup bittersweet chocolate chips

1/3 cup peanut butter chips

1. Pour the Greek yogurt, unsweetened cocoa and coffee into a large mixing bowl.

2. Whisk until it forms soft peaks. Place in the refrigerator to chill for 2 hours.

3. Add rest ingredients to a large mixing bowl.

4. Transfer to the Ninja Creami pint container.

5. Mix until smooth.

6. Select the Re-spin function if, after processing, you want your processed treat softer and creamier.

7. Spoon into individual bowls and freeze leftovers in an airtight container.

Chapter Eleven

Sugar-free Coconut Vanilla Ice Cream

Prep time: 5 minutes | Cook time: 5 minutes| Serves 2

6 frozen bananas, peeled

3 tablespoons unsweetened coconut milk

1 teaspoon pure vanilla extract

1/2 teaspoon pure coconut extract

1/2 teaspoon sugar substitute (like Stevia)

1.

Add all the ingredients to a large mixing bowl.

2. Transfer to the Ninja Creami pint container.

3. Mix until smooth.

4. Select the Re-spin function if, after processing, you want your processed treat softer and creamier.

5. Spoon into individual bowls and freeze leftovers in an airtight container.

Chapter Twelve

Chocolate Peanut Butter Banana Ice Cream

Prep time: 5 minutes | Cook time: 5 minutes| Serves 3

9 frozen bananas, peeled

2 tablespoons natural peanut butter, no sugar added

1/3 cup 85% dark cacao bar, chopped

1. Add all the ingredients to a large mixing bowl.

2. Transfer to the Ninja Creami pint container.

3. Mix until smooth.

4. Select the Re-spin function if, after processing, you want your processed treat softer and creamier.

5. Spoon into individual bowls and top with dark chocolate chunks.

6. Freeze leftovers in an airtight container.

Chapter Thirteen

Strawberry Banana Ice Cream

Prep time: 5 minutes | Cook time: 5 minutes| Serves 2

8 frozen bananas, peeled

1 cup frozen strawberries

1. Add all the ingredients to a large mixing bowl.

2.

Transfer to the Ninja Creami pint container.

3. Mix until smooth.

4. Select the Re-spin function if, after processing, you want your processed treat softer and creamier.

5. Spoon into individual bowls and freeze leftovers in an airtight container.

Chapter Fourteen

Vanilla Avocado Banana Ice Cream

Prep time: 5 minutes | Cook time: 5 minutes| Serves 3

9 frozen bananas, peeled

1 frozen avocado, peeled and pitted

1 tablespoon honey

1 teaspoon pure vanilla extract

1. Add all the ingredients to a large mixing bowl.

2. Transfer to the Ninja Creami pint container.

3. Mix until smooth.

4. Select the Re-spin function if, after processing, you want your processed treat softer and creamier.

5. Spoon into individual bowls and freeze leftovers in an airtight container.

Chapter Fifteen

Almond-Banana Ice Cream

Prep time: 5 minutes | Cook time: 5 minutes| Serves 4

12 frozen bananas, peeled

1/2 cup almond butter

2 teaspoons pure vanilla extract

1 teaspoon honey

1. Add all the ifgredients to a large mixing bowl.

2. Transfer to the Ninja Creami pint container.

3. Mix until smooth.

4. Select the Re-spin function if, after processing, you want your processed treat softer and creamier.

5. Spoon into individual bowls and freeze leftovers in an airtight container.

Chapter Sixteen

Peach Ice Cream

Prep time: 5 minutes | Cook time: 5 minutes| Serves 2

3 cups frozen peaches

1 cup Greek yogurt, vanilla flavored

1 tablespoon honey

1 cup frozen peaches, chopped

1. Add all the ingredients to a large mixing bowl.

2. Transfer to the Ninja Creami pint container.

3. Mix until smooth.

4. Select the Re-spin function if, after processing, you want your processed treat softer and creamier.

5. Fold in chopped peaches.

6. Spoon into individual bowls and freeze leftover soft-serve in an airtight container.

Chapter Seventeen

Blueberry Banana Ice Cream

Prep time: 5 minutes | Cook time: 5 minutes| Serves 5

9 frozen bananas, peeled

1 cup frozen blueberries, stemmed

2 teaspoons pure vanilla extract

1. Add all the ingredients to a large mixing bowl.

2.

Transfer to the Ninja Creami pint container.

3. Mix until smooth.

4. Select the Re-spin function if, after processing, you want your processed treat softer and creamier.

5. Fold in vanilla extract and mix until well-blended.

6. Spoon into individual bowls, and freeze leftovers in an airtight container.

Chapter Eighteen

Lemon Buttermilk Pie Ice Cream

Prep time: 5 minutes | Cook time: 5 minutes| Serves 4

9 frozen bananas, peeled

1/2 cup kefir, unsweetened and unflavored

1/4 cup Greek yogurt, vanilla flavored

3 teaspoons brown sugar substitute

3 tablespoons lemon juice

1 teaspoon lemon zest

1/2 cup frozen pie crust bits

1. Place a mixing bowl under the Yonanas chute and push the bananas through.

2. Fold the kefir, coconut cream, brown sugar, lemon juice and lemon zest into the soft-serve.

3. Transfer to the Ninja Creami pint container.

4. Mix until smooth.

5. Mix until well-blended.

6. Select the Re-spin function if, after processing, you want your processed treat softer and creamier.

7. Scoop into a cone or bowl and top with crushed pie pieces.

8. Freeze leftovers in an airtight container.

Chapter Nineteen

Watermelon Ice Cream

Prep time: 5 minutes | Cook time: 5 minutes| Serves 2

3 cups frozen watermelon, seeded

1/2 cup cream of coconut, chilled

1 teaspoon honey

1. Place the mixing bowl under the Yonanas chute and push the watermelon through the chute.

2. Add coconut cream and honey to the mixing bowl.

3. Transfer to the Ninja Creami pint container.

4. Mix until well-blended.

5. Select the Re-spin function if, after processing, you want your processed treat softer and creamier.

6. Scoop into a cone or bowl and top with crushed pie pieces.

7. Freeze leftovers in an airtight container.

Chapter Twenty

Sweet Corn Ice Cream

Prep time: 5 minutes | Cook time: 5 minutes| Serves 4

2 bags frozen corn

1/2 cup kefir, plain, frozen into cubes

1 teaspoon nonfat condensed milk, sweetened, frozen into cubes

1. Add all the ingredients to a large mixing bowl.

2. Transfer to the Ninja Creami pint container.

3. Mix until smooth.

4. Fold the kefir and nonfat condensed milk into the soft-serve until well-blended.

5. Select the Re-spin function if, after processing, you want your processed treat softer and creamier.

6. Spoon into individual bowls and freeze any leftover soft-serve in an airtight container.

Chapter Twenty-One

Pumpkin Cheesecake Ice Cream

Prep time: 10 minutes | Cook time: 5 minutes,
Freeze Time: 24 hours | Serves 1 pint

8 oz. cream cheese

1 cup heavy cream

¼ cup pumpkin puree

½ cup brown sugar

1 teaspoon vanilla Txtract

½ teaspoon pumpkin pie spice

1. Add the cream cheese to a microwave-safe bowl.

2. Microwave for 30 seconds.

3. Add the rest of the ingredients to the bowl.

4. Mix well.

5. Transfer to the Ninja Creami pint container.

6. Freeze for 24 hours.

7. Process in the machine using the Ice Cream function.

8. Select the Re-spin function if, after processing, you want your processed treat softer and creamier.

Chapter Twenty-Two

Mocha & Nut Ice Cream

Prep time: 1 minute|Freeze time: 24 hours | Serves 4

1 ¾ cups coconut cream

½ cup mocha cappuccino mix

3 tablespoons raw agave nectar

1. Mix all the ingredients in the Ninja Creami pint container.

2. Freeze for 24 hours.

3. Add the container to the machine.

4. Select Ice Cream function.

5. Select the Re-spin function if, after processing, you want your processed treat softer and creamier.

Chapter Twenty-Three

Matcha Ice Cream

Prep time: 15 minute|Freeze time: 24 hours | Serves 4

1 tablespoon cream cheese

2 tablespoons matcha powder

¾ cup heavy cream

1 teaspoon vanilla extract

1 cup milk

1/3 cup granulated sugar

1. Microwave the cream cheese for 10 seconds.

2. Stir in the rest of the ingredients.

3. Mix well.

4. Pour the mixture into your Ninja Creami pint container.

5. Freeze for 24 hours.

6. Add the container to the machine.

7. Push the Ice Cream function.

8. Select the Re-spin function if, after processing, you want your processed treat softer and creamier.

Chapter Twenty-Four

Raspberry Ice Cream

Prep time: 5 minute|Freeze time: 24 hours | Serves 4

2 tablespoons monk fruit sweetener

2 tablespoons raw agave nectar

1 cup milk

¾ cup heavy cream

½ teaspoon raspberry extract

¼ teaspoon lemon extract

½ teaspoon vanilla extract

2 drops red or pink food coloring

1. Combine all the ingredients in the Ninja Creami pint container.

2. Freeze for 24 hours.

3. Transfer the container to the machine.

4. Press the Ice Cream button.

5. Select the Re-spin function if, after processing, you want your processed treat softer and creamier.

Chapter Twenty-Five

Chapter 4 Ice Cream Mix-Ins

Sweet & Salty Ice Cream

Prep time: 10 minute|Freeze time: 24 hours | Serves 4

1 tablespoon cream cheese, softened

1 cup whole milk

3/4 cup heavy cream

1/3 cup granulated sugar

Mix-Ins

1 tablespoon potato chips

1 tablespoon mini pretzels

1 sugar cone, crushed

1. Microwave the cream cheese for 10 seconds.

2. Stir in the milk, cream and sugar.

3. Mix well.

4. Pour the mixture into your Ninja Creami pint container.

5. Freeze for 24 hours.

6. Transfer the container to the machine.

7. Push the Ice Cream button.

8.

Select the Re-spin function if, after processing, you want your processed treat softer and creamier.

Chapter Twenty-Six

Cookie & Cream with Mint Ice Cream

Prep time: 5 minute|Freeze time: 24 hours | Serves 4

¾ cup coconut cream

5 drops green food coloring

2 tablespoons raw agave nectar

1 cup oat milk

¼ cup monk fruit sweetener

½ teaspoon mint extract

Mix-Ins

3 chocolate sandwich cookies, sliced into quarters

1. Whisk the coconut cream until smooth.

2. Stir in the rest of the ingredients except the mix-in.

3. Transfer the mixture to the Ninja Creami pint container.

4. Freeze for 24 hours.

5. Process in the machine using the Ice Cream function.

6. Add the chocolate sandwich cookie slices.

7. Process using the Mix-in mode.

8. Select the Re-spin function if, after processing, you want your processed treat softer and creamier.

Chapter Twenty-Seven

Chocolate-Covered Coconut and Almond Ice Cream

Prep time: 5 minutes|Freeze time: 24 hours | Serves 4

1 (14-ounce) can full-fat unsweetened coconut milk

¼ cup unsweetened almond milk

½ cup organic sugar

1 teaspoon vanilla extract

2 tablespoons toasted almond halves

2 tablespoons vegan chocolate chips

1. In a medium bowl, whisk together the coconut milk, almond milk, sugar, and vanilla until everything is incorporated and the sugar is dissolved.

2. Pour the base into a clean CREAMi Pint. Place the storage lid on the container and freeze for 24 hours.

3. Remove the pint from the freezer and take off the lid. Place the pint in the outer bowl of your Ninja® CREAMi™, install the Creamerizer™ Paddle in the outer bowl lid, and lock the lid assembly onto the outer bowl. Place the bowl assembly on the motor base, and twist the handle to the

right to raise the platform and lock it in place. Select the Ice Cream function.

4. Once the machine has finished processing, remove the lid from the pint container. With a spoon, create a 1½-inch-wide hole that reaches the bottom of the pint. Add the almond halves and chocolate chips to the hole, then replace the lid and select the Mix-In function.

5. Once the machine has finished processing, remove the ice cream from the pint.

6. Select the Re-spin function if, after processing, you want your processed treat softer and creamier.

7. Serve immediately.

Chapter Twenty-Eight

Coffee and Cookies Ice Cream

Prep time: 5 minutes|Freeze time: 24 hours | Serves 4

1 tablespoon cream cheese, at room temperature

⅓ cup granulated sugar

1 teaspoon vanilla extract

1 tablespoon instant espresso

¾ cup heavy (whipping) cream

1 cup whole milk

¼ cup crushed chocolate sandwich cookies

1. In a large bowl, whisk together the cream cheese, sugar, and vanilla for about 1 minute, until the mixture looks like frosting.

2. Slowly whisk in the instant espresso, heavy cream, and milk until fully combined.

3. Pour the base into a clean CREAMi Pint. Place the lid on the container and freeze for 24 hours.

4. Remove the pint from the freezer and take off the lid. Place the pint in the outer bowl of your Ninja® CREAMi™, install the Creamerizer™ Paddle in the outer bowl lid, and lock the lid assembly onto the outer bowl. Place the bowl assembly on the

motor base, and twist the handle to the right to raise the platform and lock it in place. Select the Ice Cream function.

5. Once the machine has finished processing, remove the lid from the pint container. With a spoon, create a 1½-inch-wide hole that reaches the bottom of the pint. Add the crushed cookies to the hole, replace the lid, and select the Mix-In function.

6. Once the machine has finished processing, remove the ice cream from the pint.

7. Select the Re-spin function if, after processing, you want your processed treat softer and creamier.

8. Serve immediately.

Chapter Twenty-Nine

Birthday Cake Ice Cream

Prep time: 5 minutes|Freeze time: 24 hours | Serves 4

5 large egg yolks

¼ cup corn syrup

2½ tablespoons granulated sugar

⅓ cup whole milk

1 cup heavy (whipping) cream

1½ tablespoons vanilla extract

3 tablespoons vanilla cake mix

2 tablespoons rainbow-colored sprinkles

1. Fill a large bowl with ice water and set it aside.

2. In a small saucepan, whisk together the egg yolks, corn syrup, and sugar until the mixture is fully combined and the sugar is dissolved. Do not do this over heat.

3. Whisk in the milk, heavy cream, and vanilla.

4. Place the pan over medium heat. Cook, stirring constantly with a rubber spatula, until the temperature reaches 165°F to 175°F on an instant-read thermometer.

5. Remove the pan from the heat and pour the base through a fine-mesh strainer into a clean CREAMi Pint. Carefully place the container in the prepared ice water bath, making sure the water doesn't spill into the base.

6. Once the base has cooled, whisk in the vanilla cake mix until it is fully incorporated. Place the storage lid on the pint container and freeze for 24 hours.

7. Remove the pint from the freezer and take off the lid. Place the pint in the outer bowl of your Ninja® CREAMi™, install the Creamerizer™ Paddle in the outer bowl lid, and lock the lid assembly onto the outer bowl. Place the bowl assembly on the motor base, and twist the handle to the right to raise the platform and lock it in place. Select the Ice Cream function.

8. Once the machine has finished processing, remove the lid from the pint container. With a spoon, create a 1½-inch-wide hole that reaches the bottom of the pint. During this process, it is okay if your treat reaches above the Max Fill line. Add the rainbow sprinkles to the hole in the pint, replace the lid, and select the Mix-In function.

9. Once the machine has finished processing, remove the ice cream from the pint.

10. Select the Re-spin function if, after processing, you want your processed treat softer and creamier.

11. Serve immediately.

Chapter Thirty

Cinnamon Cereal Milk Ice Cream

Prep time: 5 minutes|Cook time:30 minutes | Freeze time: 24 hours | Serves 4

4 large egg yolks

1 tablespoon light corn syrup

¼ cup plus 1 tablespoon granulated sugar

⅓ cup whole milk

1 cup heavy (whipping) cream

1 teaspoon vanilla extract

3½ cups cinnamon square cereal, divided

1. Fill a large bowl with ice water and set it aside.

2. In a small saucepan, whisk together the egg yolks, corn syrup, and sugar until the mixture is fully combined and the sugar is dissolved. Do not do this over heat.

3. Whisk in the milk, heavy cream, and vanilla.

4. Place the pan over medium heat. Cook, stirring constantly with a rubber spatula, until the temperature reaches 165°F to 175°F on an instant-read thermometer. Remove the pan from the heat and stir in 3 cups of cereal. Let steep for 20 minutes.

5.

Remove the pan from the heat and pour the base through a fine-mesh strainer into a clean CREAMi Pint. Carefully place the container in the prepared ice water bath, making sure the water doesn't spill into the base.

6. Once the base has cooled, place the storage lid on the pint and freeze for 24 hours.

7. Remove the pint from the freezer and take off the lid. Place the pint in the outer bowl of your Ninja® CREAMi™, install the Creamerizer™ Paddle in the outer bowl lid, and lock the lid assembly onto the outer bowl. Place the bowl assembly on the motor base, and twist the handle to the right to raise the platform and lock it in place. Select the Ice Cream function.

8.

Once the machine has finished processing, remove the lid from the pint container. With a spoon, create a 1½-inch-wide hole that reaches the bottom of the pint. During this process, it is okay if your treat reaches above the Max Fill line. Add the remaining ¼ cup of cereal to the hole in the pint, replace the lid, and select the Mix-In function.

9. Once processing is complete, remove the ice cream from the pint.

10. Select the Re-spin function if, after processing, you want your processed treat softer and creamier.

11. Serve immediately.

Chapter Thirty-One

Triple-Chocolate Ice Cream

Prep time: 5 minutes|Cook time:10 minutes | Freeze time: 24 hours | Serves 4

4 large egg yolks

⅓ cup granulated sugar

1 tablespoon unsweetened cocoa powder

1 tablespoon hot fudge sauce

¾ cup heavy (whipping) cream

½ cup whole milk

1 teaspoon vanilla extract

¼ cup white chocolate chips

1. Fill a large bowl with ice water and set it aside.

2. In a small saucepan, whisk together the egg yolks, sugar, and cocoa powder until the mixture is fully combined and the sugar is dissolved. Do not do this over heat.

3. Whisk in the hot fudge, heavy cream, milk, and vanilla.

4. Place the pan over medium heat. Cook, stirring constantly with a rubber spatula, until the temperature reaches 165°F to 175°F on an instant-read thermometer.

5.

Remove the pan from the heat and pour the base through a fine-mesh strainer into a clean CREAMi Pint. Carefully place the container in the prepared ice water bath, making sure the water doesn't spill into the base.

6. Once the base has cooled, place the storage lid on the pint and freeze for 24 hours.

7. Remove the pint from the freezer and take off the lid. Place the pint in the outer bowl of your Ninja® CREAMi™, install the Creamerizer™ Paddle in the outer bowl lid, and lock the lid assembly onto the outer bowl. Place the bowl assembly on the motor base, and twist the handle to the right to raise the platform and lock it in place. Select the Ice Cream function.

8.

Once the machine has finished processing, remove the lid from the pint container. With a spoon, create a 1½-inch-wide hole that reaches the bottom of the pint. During this process, it is okay if your treat reaches above the Max Fill line. Add the white chocolate chips to the hole in the pint, replace the lid, and select the Mix-In function.

9. Once the machine has finished processing, remove the ice cream from the pint.

10. Select the Re-spin function if, after processing, you want your processed treat softer and creamier.

11. Serve immediately with desired toppings.

Chapter Thirty-Two

Bourbon-Maple-Walnut Ice Cream

Prep time: 5 minutes|Cook time:10 minutes | Freeze time: 24 hours | Serves 4

4 large egg yolks

¼ cup maple syrup

¼ cup corn syrup

2 tablespoons bourbon

½ cup whole milk

1 cup heavy (whipping) cream

¼ cup toasted walnut halves

1. Fill a large bowl with ice water and set it aside.

2. In a small saucepan, whisk together the egg yolks, maple syrup, corn syrup, and bourbon until the mixture is fully combined. Do not do this over heat.

3. Whisk in the milk and heavy cream.

4. Place the pan over medium heat. Cook, stirring constantly with a rubber spatula, until the temperature reaches 165°F to 175°F on an instant-read thermometer.

5. Remove the pan from the heat and pour the base into a clean CREAMi Pint. Carefully place the container in the prepared

ice water bath, making sure the water doesn't spill into the base.

6. Once the base has cooled, place the storage lid on the pint and freeze for 24 hours.

7. Remove the pint from the freezer and take off the lid. Place the pint in the outer bowl of your Ninja® CREAMi™, install the Creamerizer™ Paddle in the outer bowl lid, and lock the lid assembly onto the outer bowl. Place the bowl assembly on the motor base, and twist the handle to the right to raise the platform and lock it in place. Select the Ice Cream function.

8. Once the machine has finished processing, remove the lid from the pint container. With a spoon, create a 1½-inch-wide hole that reaches the bottom of the pint. During this process, it is okay if your treat reaches

above the Max Fill line. Add the toasted walnuts to the hole in the pint, replace the lid, and select the Mix-In function.

9. Once the machine has finished processing, remove the ice cream from the pint.

10. Select the Re-spin function if, after processing, you want your processed treat softer and creamier.

11. Serve immediately.

Chapter Thirty-Three

Cookies and Coconut Ice Cream

Prep time: 5 minutes | Freeze time: 24 hours | Serves 4

1 (14-ounce) can full-fat unsweetened coconut milk

½ cup organic sugar

1 teaspoon vanilla extract

4 chocolate sandwich cookies, crushed

1. In a medium bowl, whisk together the coconut milk, sugar, and vanilla until well combined and the sugar is dissolved.

2. Pour the base into a clean CREAMi Pint. Place the storage lid on the container and freeze for 24 hours.

3. Remove the pint from the freezer and take off the lid. Place the pint in the outer bowl of your Ninja® CREAMi™, install the Creamerizer™ Paddle in the outer bowl lid, and lock the lid assembly onto the outer bowl. Place the bowl assembly on the motor base, and twist the handle to the right to raise the platform and lock it in place. Select the Ice Cream function.

4. Once the machine has finished processing, remove the lid from the pint container.

With a spoon, create a 1½-inch-wide hole that reaches the bottom of the pint. During this process, it is okay if your treat reaches above the Max Fill line. Add the crushed cookies to the hole in the pint, replace the lid, and select the Mix-In function.

5. Once the machine has finished processing, remove the ice cream from the pint.

6. Select the Re-spin function if, after processing, you want your processed treat softer and creamier.

7. Serve immediately with desired toppings.

Chapter Thirty-Four

Sneaky Mint Chip Ice Cream

Prep time: 5 minutes|Cook time:5 minutes | Freeze time: 24 hours | Serves 4

3 large egg yolks

1 tablespoon corn syrup

¼ cup granulated sugar

⅓ cup whole milk

¾ cup heavy (whipping) cream

1 cup packed fresh spinach

½ cup frozen peas, thawed

1 teaspoon mint extract

¼ cup semisweet chocolate chips

1. Fill a large bowl with ice water and set it aside.

2. In a small saucepan, whisk together the egg yolks, corn syrup, and sugar until the mixture is fully combined and the sugar is dissolved. Do not do this over heat.

3. Whisk in the milk and heavy cream.

4. Place the pan over medium heat. Cook, stirring constantly with a rubber spatula, until the temperature reaches 165°F to 175°F on an instant-read thermometer.

5.

Remove the pan from the heat and pour the base into a clean CREAMi Pint. Carefully place the container in the prepared ice water bath, making sure the water doesn't spill into the base.

6. Once the mixture has completely cooled, pour the base into a blender and add the spinach, peas, and mint extract. Blend on high for 30 seconds. Strain the base through a fine-mesh strainer back into the CREAMi Pint. Place the storage lid on the container and freeze for 24 hours.

7. Remove the pint from the freezer and take off the lid. Place the pint in the outer bowl of your Ninja® CREAMi™, install the Creamerizer™ Paddle in the outer bowl lid, and lock the lid assembly onto the outer bowl. Place the bowl assembly on the motor base, and twist the handle to the

right to raise the platform and lock it in place. Select the Ice Cream function.

8. Once the machine has finished processing, remove the lid from the pint container. With a spoon, create a 1½-inch-wide hole that reaches the bottom of the pint. During this process, it is okay if your treat reaches above the Max Fill line. Add the chocolate chips to the hole in the pint, replace the lid, and select the Mix-In function.

9. Once the machine has finished processing, remove the ice cream from the pint.

10. Select the Re-spin function if, after processing, you want your processed treat softer and creamier.

11. Serve immediately.

Chapter Thirty-Five

Coconut Mint Chip Ice Cream

Prep time: 5 minutes| Freeze time: 24 hours | Serves 4

1 (14-ounce) can full-fat unsweetened coconut milk

½ cup organic sugar

½ teaspoon mint extract

¼ cup mini vegan chocolate chips

1. In a medium bowl, whisk together the coconut milk, sugar, and mint extract until everything is well combined and the sugar is dissolved.

2. Pour the base into a clean CREAMi Pint. Place the storage lid on the container and freeze for 24 hours.

3. Remove the pint from the freezer and take off the lid. Place the pint in the outer bowl of your Ninja® CREAMi™, install the Creamerizer™ Paddle in the outer bowl lid, and lock the lid assembly onto the outer bowl. Place the bowl assembly on the motor base, and twist the handle to the right to raise the platform and lock it in place. Select the Ice Cream function.

4. Once the machine has finished processing, remove the lid from the pint contain-

er. With a spoon, create a 1½-inch-wide hole that reaches the bottom of the pint. During this process, it is okay if your treat reaches above the Max Fill line. Add the mini chocolate chips to the hole in the pint, replace the lid, and select the Mix-In function.

5. Once the machine has finished processing, remove the ice cream from the pint.

6. Select the Re-spin function if, after processing, you want your processed treat softer and creamier.

7. Serve immediately with desired toppings.

Chapter Thirty-Six

Sweet Potato Pie Ice Cream

Prep time: 5 minutes| Freeze time: 24 hours | Serves 4

1 cup canned pureed sweet potato

1 tablespoon corn syrup

¼ cup plus 1 tablespoon light brown sugar

1 teaspoon vanilla extract

1 teaspoon cinnamon

¾ cup heavy (whipping) cream

¼ cup mini marshmallows

1. Combine the sweet potato puree, corn syrup, brown sugar, vanilla, and cinnamon in a blender. Blend on high until smooth.

2. Pour the base into a clean CREAMi Pint. Whisk in the heavy cream until combined. Place the storage lid on the container and freeze for 24 hours.

3. Remove the pint from the freezer and take off the lid. Place the pint in the outer bowl of your Ninja® CREAMi™, install the Creamerizer™ Paddle in the outer bowl lid, and lock the lid assembly onto the outer bowl. Place the bowl assembly on the motor base, and twist the handle to the right to raise the platform and lock it in place. Select the Ice Cream function.

4. Once the machine has finished processing, remove the lid from the pint container. With a spoon, create a 1½-inch-wide hole that reaches the bottom of the pint. During this process, it is okay if your treat reaches above the Max Fill line. Add the marshmallows to the hole in the pint, replace the lid, and select the Mix-In function.

5. Once the machine has finished processing, remove the ice cream from the pint.

6. Select the Re-spin function if, after processing, you want your processed treat softer and creamier.

7. Serve immediately with desired toppings.

Chapter Thirty-Seven

Vanilla Pecan Ice Cream

Prep time: 10 minutes | Cook time: 5 minutes| Serves 6

1 cup whole milk

¾ cup heavy cream

⅓ cup granulated sugar

½ cup toasted pecans, coarsely chopped

5 pecan shortbread cookies

½ cup potato chips, crushed

1. Place all the ingredients in a blender. Mix well until smooth.

2. Pour the mixture into the Ninja CREAMi Pint and close it with the lid.

3. Place the pint into the freezer and freeze for 24 hours.

4. Once done, remove the lid and place the pint into the outer bowl of the Ninja CREAMi. Secure the Creamerizer Paddle into the outer bowl.

5. Lock the lid by rotating it clockwise.

6. Turn on the unit and press the ICE CREAM button.

7. Once done, take out the bowl from the Ninja CREAMi.

8.

Select the Re-spin function if, after processing, you want your processed treat softer and creamier.

9. Serve immediately.

Chapter Thirty-Eight

Vanilla Blueberry Ice Cream

Prep time: 5 minutes | Cook time: 5 minutes|
Serves 4

1 cup whole milk

¾ cup heavy cream

⅓ cup granulated sugar

1 large egg, beaten

½ cup frozen blueberries, thawed

1. Place the ingredients in a blender. Mix well until smooth.

2. Pour the mixture into the Ninja CREAMi Pint and close it with the lid.

3. Place the pint into the freezer for 24 hours.

4. Once frozen, remove the lid and set the pint into the outer bowl of the Ninja CREAMi. Set the Creamerizer Paddle into the outer bowl.

5. Lock the lid by rotating it clockwise.

6. Turn the unit on and then press the ICE CREAM button.

7. Once done, take out the bowl from the Ninja CREAMi.

8.

Select the Re-spin function if, after processing, you want your processed treat softer and creamier.

9. Serve immediately.

Chapter Thirty-Nine

Chocolate Nut Ice Cream

Prep time: 5 minutes | Cook time: 5 minutes| Serves 4

1 cup whole milk

¾ cup heavy cream

⅓ cup granulated sugar

2 tablespoons mini chocolate chips

2 tablespoons cocoa powder

½ cup brownies, Chopped

½ cup walnuts, chopped

1. Place the ingredients in a blender. Mix well until smooth.

2. Pour the mixture into the Ninja CREAMi Pint and close it with the lid.

3. Place the pint into the freezer and freeze for 24 hours.

4. Once done, open the lid and set the pint into the outer bowl of the Ninja CREAMi. Place the Creamerizer Paddle into the outer bowl.

5. Lock the lid by rotating it clockwise.

6. Turn on the unit and then press the ICE CREAM button.

7. Once done, take out the bowl from the Ninja CREAMi.

8. Select the Re-spin function if, after processing, you want your processed treat softer and creamier.

9. Serve immediately.

Chapter Forty

Vanilla Peanut Butter Ice Cream

Prep time: 5 minutes | Cook time: 5 minutes| Serves 4

½ cup peanut butter cups, chopped

¼ cup peanut butter chips

½ cup salted pretzels, crushed

1 cup whole milk

¾ cup heavy cream

⅓ cup granulated sugar

1. Add the ingredients to a blender. Mix well until smooth.

2. Pour the mixture into the Ninja CREAMi Pint and close it with the lid.

3. Place the pint into the freezer and freeze for 24 hours.

4. Once done, open the lid and set the pint into the outer bowl of the Ninja CREAMi. Put the Creamerizer Paddle into the outer bowl.

5. Lock the lid by rotating it clockwise.

6. Turn on the unit and press the ICE CREAM button.

7. Once done, take out the bowl from the Ninja CREAMi.

8.

Select the Re-spin function if, after processing, you want your processed treat softer and creamier.

9. Serve immediately.

Chapter Forty-One

Cookies & Cream Ice Cream

Prep time: 5 minutes | Cook time: **24 Hours and 5 Minutes** | Serves 2

½ tablespoon cream cheese, softened

¼ cup granulated sugar

½ teaspoon vanilla extract

½ cup heavy cream

½ cup whole milk

1½ chocolate sandwich cookies, broken, for mix-in

1. Microwave the cream cheese for 10 seconds in a large microwave-safe bowl. Combine the sugar and vanilla extract in a mixing bowl and whisk or scrape together until the mixture resembles frosting, about 60 seconds.

2. Slowly whisk in the heavy cream and milk until smooth and the sugar has dissolved.

3. Pour the base into an empty CREAMi Pint. Place storage lid on the Pint and freeze for 24 hours.

4. Remove the Pint from the freezer and remove the lid from the Pint. Place the Pint in the outer bowl, install Creamerizer Paddle onto the outer bowl lid, and lock the lid assembly on the outer bowl. Select ICE CREAM.

5. With a spoon, create a 1½-inch wide hole that reaches the bottom of the Pint. During this process, it's okay for your treat to go above the max fill line. Add the broken chocolate sandwich cookies to the hole and process again using the MIX-IN program.

6. When processing is complete, remove the ice cream from the Pint.

7. Select the Re-spin function if, after processing, you want your processed treat softer and creamier.

8. Serve immediately.

Chapter Forty-Two

Cinnamon Sugar Cookie Ice Cream

Prep time: 5 minutes | Cook time: 5 minutes| Serves 4

3 to 6 sugar cookies

½ teaspoon ground cinnamon

1 cup whole milk

¾ cup heavy cream

⅓ cup granulated sugar

1. Take a blender and add the ingredients to it. Mix well until smooth.

2. Pour the mixture into the Ninja CREAMi Pint and close the lid.

3. Place the pint into the freezer and freeze for 24 hours.

4. Once done, open the lid and place the pint into the outer bowl of the Ninja CREAMi. Set the Creamerizer Paddle into the outer bowl.

5. Lock the lid by rotating it clockwise.

6. Turn on the unit and then press the ICE CREAM button.

7. Once done, take out the bowl from the Ninja CREAMi.

8.

Select the Re-spin function if, after processing, you want your processed treat softer and creamier.

9. Serve immediately.

Chapter Forty-Three

Mint Cookies Ice Cream

Prep time: 5 minutes | Cook time: 15 minutes| Serves 4

¾ cup coconut cream

¼ cup monk fruit sweetener with Erythritol

2 tablespoons agave nectar

½ teaspoon mint extract

5-6 drops green food coloring

1 cup oat milk

3 chocolate sandwich cookies, quartered

1. In a large bowl, add the coconut cream and beat until smooth.

2. Add the sweetener, agave nectar, mint extract and food coloring and beat until sweetener is dissolved.

3. Add the oat milk and beat until well combined.

4. Transfer the mixture into an empty Ninja CREAMi pint container.

5. Cover the container with storage lid and freeze for 24 hours.

6. After 24 hours, remove the lid from container and arrange into the Outer Bowl of Ninja CREAMi.

7.

Install the Creamerizer Paddle onto the lid of Outer Bowl.

8. Then rotate the lid clockwise to lock.

9. Press Power button to turn on the unit.

10. Then press Lite Ice Cream button.

11. When the program is completed, with a spoon, create a 1½-inch wide hole in the center that reaches the bottom of the pint container.

12. Add the cookie pieces into the hole and press Mix-In button.

13. When the program is completed, turn the Outer Bowl and release it from the machine.

14. Transfer the ice cream into serving bowls.

15.

Select the Re-spin function if, after processing, you want your processed treat softer and creamier.

16. Serve immediately.

Chapter Forty-Four

Jelly & Peanut Butter Ice Cream

Prep time: 5 minutes | Cook time: 5 minutes| Serves 4

3 tablespoons granulated sugar

4 large egg yolks

1 cup whole milk

⅓ cup heavy cream

¼ cup smooth peanut butter

3 tablespoons grape jelly

¼ cup honey roasted peanuts, chopped

1. In a small saucepan, add the sugar and egg yolks and beat until sugar is dissolved.

2. Add the milk, heavy cream, peanut butter, and grape jelly to the saucepan and stir to combine.

3. Place saucepan over medium heat and cook until temperature reaches cook until temperature reaches to 165 -175° F, stirring continuously with a rubber spatula.

4. Remove from the heat and through a fine-mesh strainer, strain the mixture into an empty Ninja CREAMi pint container.

5. Place the container into ice bath to cool.

6. After cooling, cover the container with storage lid and freeze for 24 hours.

7. After 24 hours, remove the lid from container and arrange into the Outer Bowl of Ninja CREAMi.

8. Install the Creamerizer Paddle onto the lid of Outer Bowl.

9. Then rotate the lid clockwise to lock.

10. Press Power button to turn on the unit.

11. Then press ICE CREAM button.

12. When the program is completed, with a spoon, create a 1½-inch wide hole in the center that reaches the bottom of the pint container.

13. Add the peanuts into the hole and press Mix-In button.

14.

When the program is completed, turn the Outer Bowl and release it from the machine.

15. Transfer the ice cream into serving bowls.

16. Select the Re-spin function if, after processing, you want your processed treat softer and creamier.

17. Serve immediately.

Chapter Forty-Five

Snack Mix Ice Cream

Prep time: 5 minutes | Cook time: 15 minutes| Serves 4

1 tablespoon cream cheese, softened

⅓ cup granulated sugar

½ teaspoon vanilla extract

1 cup whole milk

¾ cup heavy cream

2 tablespoons sugar cone pieces

1 tablespoon mini pretzels

1 tablespoon potato chips, crushed

1. 1n a large microwave-safe bowl, add the cream cheese and microwave on High for about ten seconds.

2. Remove from the microwave and stir until smooth.

3. Add the sugar and vanilla extract and with a wire whisk, beat until the mixture looks like frosting.

4. Slowly add the milk and heavy cream and beat until well combined.

5. Transfer the mixture into an empty Ninja CREAMi pint container.

6. Cover the container with storage lid and freeze for 24 hours.

7. After 24 hours, remove the lid from container and arrange into the Outer Bowl of Ninja CREAMi.

8. Install the Creamerizer Paddle onto the lid of Outer Bowl.

9. Then rotate the lid clockwise to lock.

10. Press Power button to turn on the unit.

11. Then press Ice Cream button.

12. When the program is completed, with a spoon, create a 1½-inch wide hole in the center that reaches the bottom of the pint container.

13. Add the cone pieces, pretzels and potato chips into the hole and press Mix-In button.

14.

When the program is completed, turn the Outer Bowl and release it from the machine.

15. Transfer the ice cream into serving bowls.

16. Select the Re-spin function if, after processing, you want your processed treat softer and creamier.

17. Serve immediately.

Chapter Forty-Six

Coffee Chip Ice Cream

Prep time: 5 minutes | Cook time: 5 minutes| Serves 4

¾ cup heavy cream

¼ cup monk fruit sweetener with Erythritol

½ teaspoon stevia sweetener

1½ tablespoons instant coffee granules

1 cup unsweetened almond milk

1 teaspoon vanilla extract

3 tablespoons chocolate chips

1 tablespoon walnuts, chopped

1. In a bowl, add the heavy cream and beat until smooth.

2. Add the remaining ingredients except for chocolate chips and walnuts and beat sweetener is dissolved.

3. Transfer the mixture into an empty Ninja CREAMi pint container.

4. Cover the container with storage lid and freeze for 24 hours.

5. After 24 hours, remove the lid from container and arrange into the Outer Bowl of Ninja CREAMi.

6. Install the Creamerizer Paddle onto the lid of Outer Bowl.

7. Then rotate the lid clockwise to lock.

8. Press Power button to turn on the unit.

9. Then press Lite Ice Cream button.

10. When the program is completed, with a spoon, create a 1½-inch wide hole in the center that reaches the bottom of the pint container.

11. Add the chocolate chips and walnuts into the hole and press Mix-In button.

12. When the program is completed, turn the Outer Bowl and release it from the machine.

13. Transfer the ice cream into serving bowls.

14. Select the Re-spin function if, after processing, you want your processed treat softer and creamier.

15. Serve immediately.

Chapter Forty-Seven

Chocolate Brownie Ice Cream

Prep time: 15 minutes | Cook time: 5 minutes| Serves 4

1 tablespoon cream cheese, softened

⅓ cup granulated sugar

1 teaspoon vanilla extract

2 tablespoons cocoa powder

1 cup whole milk

¾ cup heavy cream

2 tablespoons mini chocolate chips

2 tablespoons brownie chunks

1. In a large microwave-safe bowl, add the cream cheese and microwave on High for about ten seconds.

2. Remove from the microwave and stir until smooth.

3. Add the sugar and almond extract and with a wire whisk, beat until the mixture looks like frosting.

4. Slowly add the milk and heavy cream and beat until well combined.

5. Transfer the mixture into an empty Ninja CREAMi pint container.

6. Cover the container with storage lid and freeze for 24 hours.

7. After 24 hours, remove the lid from container and arrange into the Outer Bowl of Ninja CREAMi.

8. Install the Creamerizer Paddle onto the lid of Outer Bowl.

9. Then rotate the lid clockwise to lock.

10. Press Power button to turn on the unit.

11. Then press Ice Cream button.

12. When the program is completed, with a spoon, create a 1½-inch wide hole in the center that reaches the bottom of the pint container.

13. Add the chocolate chunks and brownie pieces into the hole and press Mix-In button.

14.

When the program is completed, turn the Outer Bowl and release it from the machine.

15. Transfer the ice cream into serving bowls.

16. Select the Re-spin function if, after processing, you want your processed treat softer and creamier.

17. Serve immediately.

Chapter Forty-Eight

Fruity Cereal Ice Cream

Prep time: 25 minutes | Cook time: **24 Hours and 30 Minutes** | Serves 2

¾ cup whole milk

1 cup fruity cereal, divided

1 tablespoon Philadelphia cream cheese, softened

¼ cup granulated sugar

1 teaspoon vanilla extract

½ cup heavy cream

1. In a large mixing bowl, combine ½ cup of the fruity cereal and the milk. Allow the mixture to settle for 15–30 minutes, stirring occasionally to infuse the milk with the fruity taste.

2. Microwave the Philadelphia cream cheese for 10 seconds in a second large microwave-safe dish. Combine the sugar and vanilla extract in a mixing bowl with a whisk or rubber spatula until the mixture resembles frosting, about 60 seconds.

3. After 15 to 30 minutes, sift the milk and cereal into the bowl with the sugar mixture using a fine-mesh filter. To release extra milk, press on the cereal with a spoon, then discard it. Mix in the heavy cream until everything is thoroughly mixed.

4. Pour the mixture into an empty ninja CREAMi Pint container. Add the strawberries to the Pint, making sure not to go over the max fill line, and freeze for 24 hours.

5. After 24 hours, remove the Pint from the freezer. Remove the lid.

6. Place the Ninja CREAMi Pint into the outer bowl. Place the outer bowl with the Pint in it into the ninja CREAMi machine and turn until the outer bowl locks into place. Push the ICE CREAM button. During the ICE CREAM function, the ice cream will mix together and become very creamy.

7. Use a spoon to create a 1½-inch wide hole that reaches the bottom of the Pint. Add the remaining ½ cup of fruity cereal to the hole and process again using the mix-in.

When processing is complete, remove the ice cream from the Pint.

8. Select the Re-spin function if, after processing, you want your processed treat softer and creamier.

9. Serve immediately.

Chapter Forty-Nine

Lite Chocolate Cookie Ice Cream

Prep time: 5 minutes | Cook time: **24 Hours and 5 Minutes** | Serves 2

1 tablespoon cream cheese, at room temperature

2 tablespoons unsweetened cocoa powder

½ teaspoon stevia sweetener

3 tablespoons raw agave nectar

1 teaspoon vanilla extract

¾ cup heavy cream

1 cup whole milk

¼ cup crushed reduced-fat sugar cookies

1. Place the cream cheese in a large microwave-safe bowl and heat on high for 10 seconds.

2. Mix in the cocoa powder, stevia, agave, and vanilla. Microwave for 60 seconds more, or until the mixture resembles frosting.

3. Slowly whisk in the heavy cream and milk until the sugar has dissolved and the mixture is thoroughly mixed.

4. Pour the base into a clean CREAMi Pint. Place the storage lid on the container and freeze for 24 hours.

5. Remove the Pint from the freezer and take off the lid. Place the Pint in the outer

bowl of your Ninja CREAMi, install the Creamerizer Paddle in the outer bowl lid, and lock the lid assembly onto the outer bowl. Place the bowl assembly on the motor base, and twist the handle to the right to raise the platform and lock it in place. Select the LITE ICE CREAM function.

6. Once the machine has finished processing, remove the lid. With a spoon, create a 1½-inch-wide hole that reaches the bottom of the Pint. During this process, it's okay if your treat goes above the max fill line. Add the crushed cookies to the hole in the Pint. Replace the Pint lid and select the MIX-IN function.

7. Once the machine has finished processing, remove the ice cream from the Pint.

8.

Select the Re-spin function if, after processing, you want your processed treat softer and creamier.

9. Serve immediately.

Chapter Fifty

Chapter 5 Sorbets

Mojito Sorbet

Prep time: 5 minutes | Cook time: 5 minutes| Serves 4

6 frozen bananas, peeled

5 sprigs of mint, chopped

3 tablespoons freshly-squeezed lime juice

3 tablespoons dark rum

1 teaspoon lime zest

1. Add all the ingredients to a large mixing bowl.

2. Transfer to the Ninja Creami pint container.

3. Mix until smooth.

4. Select the Re-spin function if, after processing, you want your processed treat softer and creamier.

5. Select the Re-spin function if, after processing, you want your processed treat softer and creamier.

6. Spoon into individual bowls and freeze leftovers in an airtight container.

Chapter Fifty-One

Apple Sorbet

Prep time: 5 minutes | Cook time: 5 minutes| Serves 3

5 frozen apples, peeled, cored and deseeded

3 tablespoons fresh pressed apple juice

1/2 teaspoon lemon juice

1. Add all the ingredients to a large mixing bowl.

2.

Transfer to the Ninja Creami pint container.

3. Mix until smooth.

4. Select the Re-spin function if, after processing, you want your processed treat softer and creamier.

5. Spoon into individual bowls and freeze leftovers in an airtight container.

Chapter Fifty-Two

Red Plum Sorbet

Prep time: 5 minutes | Cook time: 5 minutes|
Serves 4

9 frozen plums, pitted and quartered

1/3 teaspoon cardamom powder

3 tablespoons of honey

1 teaspoon lemon juice

1. Add all the ingredients to a large mixing
   bowl.

2. Transfer to the Ninja Creami pint container.

3. Mix until smooth.

4. Select the Re-spin function if, after processing, you want your processed treat softer and creamier.

5. Spoon into individual bowls and freeze leftovers in an airtight container.

Chapter Fifty-Three

Watermelon Lime Sorbet

Prep time: 5 minutes | Cook time: 5 minutes| Serves 4

3½ cups seedless watermelon chunks

2 teaspoons lime juice

¼ cup warm water

1. Place all the ingredients in a blender. Mix well until smooth.

2.

Pour the mixture into the Ninja CREAMi Pint and close the lid.

3. Place the pint into the freezer and freeze for 24 hours.

4. Once done, open the lid and place the pint into the outer bowl of the Ninja CREAMi. Set the Creamerizer Paddle into the outer bowl.

5. Lock the lid by rotating it clockwise.

6. Turn on the unit and press the SORBET button.

7. Once done, take out the bowl from the Ninja CREAMi.

8. Select the Re-spin function if, after processing, you want your processed treat softer and creamier.

9. Serve and enjoy your yummy sorbet.

Chapter Fifty-Four

Banana Sorbet

Prep time: 5 minutes | Cook time: 5 minutes|
Serves 4

2 large bananas

Water, as required

1. Place the ingredients in a blender. Mix well until smooth.

2. Pour the mixture into the Ninja CREAMi Pint and close it with the lid.

3. Place the pint into the freezer and freeze for 24 hours.

4. Once done, open the lid and place the pint into the outer bowl of the Ninja CREAMi. Set the Creamerizer Paddle into the outer bowl.

5. Lock the lid by rotating it clockwise.

6. Turn on the unit and press the SORBET button.

7. Once done, take out the bowl from the Ninja CREAMi.

8. Select the Re-spin function if, after processing, you want your processed treat softer and creamier.

9. Serve and enjoy this yummy sorbet.

Chapter Fifty-Five

Honey Blueberry Lemon Sorbet

Prep time: 5 minutes | Cook time: 5 minutes| Serves 4

3 cups fresh blueberries

2 tablespoons raw honey

3 tablespoons lemon juice

1 teaspoon lemon zest

⅓ cup water

1.

Add the ingredients to a blender. Mix well until smooth.

2. Pour the mixture into the Ninja CREAMi Pint and close it with the lid.

3. Place the pint into the freezer and freeze for 24 hours.

4. Once done, open the lid and place the pint into the outer bowl of the Ninja CREAMi. Set the Creamerizer Paddle into the outer bowl.

5. Lock the lid by rotating it clockwise.

6. Turn the unit on and press the SORBET button.

7. Once done, take out the bowl from the Ninja CREAMi.

8.

Select the Re-spin function if, after processing, you want your processed treat softer and creamier.

9. Serve and enjoy this yummy sorbet.

Chapter Fifty-Six

Pineapple Basil Sorbet

Prep time: 5 minutes | Cook time: 5 minutes| Serves 4

16 ounces canned pineapple chunks, with juice

1 teaspoon lemon juice

1 teaspoon lemon zest

1 small piece of ginger, sliced

1 teaspoon basil leaves

⅓ cup white caster sugar

1. Place all the ingredients in a blender. Mix well until smooth.

2. Pour the mixture into the Ninja CREAMi Pint and close the lid.

3. Place the pint into the freezer and freeze for 24 hours.

4. Once done, open the lid, place the pint into the outer bowl of the Ninja CREAMi, and set the Creamerizer Paddle into the outer bowl.

5. Lock the lid by rotating it clockwise.

6. Turn the unit on and press the SORBET button.

7. Once done, take out the bowl from the Ninja CREAMi.

8.

Select the Re-spin function if, after processing, you want your processed treat softer and creamier.

9. Serve and enjoy this yummy sorbet.

Chapter Fifty-Seven

Vanilla Rhubarb Sorbet

Prep time: 5 minutes | Cook time: 5 minutes| Serves 4

3 cups rhubarb, chopped

½ teaspoon vanilla extract

2/3 cup golden caster sugar

3 tablespoons liquid glucose

2 teaspoons star anise

1 cup lemon juice

1. Add the ingredients to a blender. Mix well until smooth.

2. Pour the mixture into the Ninja CREAMi Pint and close the lid.

3. Place the pint into the freezer and freeze for 24 hours.

4. Once done, open the lid and place the pint into the outer bowl of the Ninja CREAMi. Set the Creamerizer Paddle into the outer bowl.

5. Lock the lid by rotating it clockwise.

6. Turn the unit on and press the SORBET button.

7. Once done, take out the bowl from the Ninja CREAMi.

8. Select the Re-spin function if, after processing, you want your processed treat softer and creamier.

9. Serve and enjoy this yummy sorbet.

Chapter Fifty-Eight

Coconut Mango Sorbet

Prep time: 5 minutes | Cook time: 5 minutes| Serves 4

3 ripe mangoes, sliced

2 tablespoons lemon juice

1 tablespoon lemon zest

3 cups dairy-free coconut milk ice cream

A few mint leaves

1.

Add all the ingredients to a blender. Mix well until smooth.

2. Pour the mixture into the Ninja CREAMi Pint and close the lid.

3. Place the pint into the freezer and freeze for 24 hours.

4. Once done, open the lid and place the pint into the outer bowl of the Ninja CREAMi. Set the Creamerizer Paddle into the outer bowl.

5. Lock the lid by rotating it clockwise.

6. Turn the unit on and press the SORBET button.

7. Once done, take out the bowl from the Ninja CREAMi.

8.

Select the Re-spin function if, after processing, you want your processed treat softer and creamier.

9. Serve and enjoy this yummy sorbet.

Smoothie bowls

Banana Smoothie Bowl

Prep time: 10 minutes | Cook time: 1 minute | Makes 2 servings

½ cup water

¼ cup quick oats

1 cup vanilla Greek yogurt

½ cup banana, peeled and sliced

3 tablespoons honey

1. In a small microwave-safe bowl, add the water and oats and microwave on High for about 1 minute

2. Remove from the microwave and stir in the yogurt, banana and honey until well combined.

3. Transfer the mixture into an empty Ninja CREAMi pint container.

4. Cover the container with storage lid and freeze for 24 hours.

5. After 24 hours, remove the lid from container and arrange into the outer bowl of Ninja CREAMi.

6. Install the "Creamerizer Paddle" onto the lid of outer bowl.

7. Then rotate the lid clockwise to lock.

8. Press "Power" button to turn on the unit.

9. Then press "SMOOTHIE BOWL" button.

10. When the program is completed, turn the outer bowl and release it from the machine.

11. Select the Re-spin function if, after processing, you want your processed treat softer and creamier.

12. Transfer the smoothie into serving bowls and serve with your favorite topping.

Chapter Fifty-Nine

Banana Rum Smoothie Bowl

Prep time: 10 minutes | Makes 2 servings

½ of ripe banana, peeled and cut in ½-inch pieces

¼ cup coconut rum

¼ cup unsweetened coconut cream

½ cup unsweetened canned coconut milk

¾ cup pineapple juice

2 tablespoons fresh lime juice

1. In a large bowl, add all the ingredients and beat until well combined.

2. Transfer the mixture into an empty Ninja CREAMi pint container.

3. Cover the container with the storage lid and freeze for 24 hours.

4. After 24 hours, remove the lid from container and arrange into the outer bowl of Ninja CREAMi.

5. Install the "Creamerizer Paddle" onto the lid of outer bowl.

6. Then rotate the lid clockwise to lock.

7. Press "Power" button to turn on the unit.

8.

Then press "SMOOTHIE BOWL" button.

9. When the program is completed, turn the outer bowl and release it from the machine.

10. Select the Re-spin function if, after processing, you want your processed treat softer and creamier.

11. Transfer the smoothie into serving bowl sand serve immediately.

Chapter Sixty

Mango Smoothie Bowl

Prep time: 10 minutes | Makes 4 servings

2 cups ripe mango, peeled, pitted and cut into 1-inch pieces

1 (14-ounce / 397-g) can unsweetened coconut milk

1.

Place the mango pieces into an empty Ninja CREAMi pint container.

2. Top with coconut milk and stir to combine.

3. Cover the container with storage lid and freeze for 24 hours.

4. After 24 hours, remove the lid from container and arrange into the outer bowl of Ninja CREAMi.

5. Install the "Creamerizer Paddle" onto the lid of outer bowl.

6. Then rotate the lid clockwise to lock.

7. Press "Power" button to turn on the unit.

8. Then press "SMOOTHIE BOWL" button.

9.

When the program is completed, turn the outer bowl and release it from the machine.

10. Select the Re-spin function if, after processing, you want your processed treat softer and creamier.

11. Transfer the smoothie into serving bowls and serve immediately.

Chapter Sixty-One

Peach and Grapefruit Smoothie Bowl

Prep time: 10 minutes | Makes 2 servings

1 cup frozen peach pieces

1 cup vanilla Greek yogurt

¼ cup fresh grapefruit juice

2 tablespoons honey

¼ teaspoon vanilla extract

½ teaspoon ground cinnamon

1. In a high-speed blender, add all ingredients and pulse until smooth

2. Transfer the mixture into an empty Ninja CREAMi pint container.

3. Cover the container with the storage lid and freeze for 24 hours.

4. After 24 hours, remove the lid from container and arrange into the outer bowl of Ninja CREAMi.

5. Install the "Creamerizer Paddle" onto the lid of outer bowl.

6. Then rotate the lid clockwise to lock.

7. Press "Power" button to turn on the unit.

8. Then press "SMOOTHIE BOWL" button.

9. When the program is completed, turn the outer bowl and release it from the machine.

10. Select the Re-spin function if, after processing, you want your processed treat softer and creamier.

11. Transfer the smoothie into serving bowls and serve immediately.

Chapter Sixty-Two

Strawberry Smoothie Bowl

Prep time: 10 minutes | Makes 4 servings

2 tablespoons vanilla protein powder

¼ cup agave nectar

¼ cup pineapple juice

½ cup whole milk

1 cup ripe banana, peeled and cut in ½-inch pieces

1 cup fresh strawberries, hulled and quartered

1. In a large bowl, add the protein powder, agave nectar, pineapple juice and milk and beat until well combined.

2. Place the banana and strawberry into an empty Ninja CREAMi pint container and with the back of a spoon, firmly press the fruit below the MAX FILL line.

3. Top with milk mixture and mix until well combined.

4. Cover the container with storage lid and freeze for 24 hours.

5. After 24 hours, remove the lid from container and arrange into the outer bowl of Ninja CREAMi.

6.

Install the "Creamerizer Paddle" onto the lid of outer bowl.

7. Then rotate the lid clockwise to lock.

8. Press "Power" button to turn on the unit.

9. Then press "SMOOTHIE BOWL" button.

10. When the program is completed, turn the outer bowl and release it from the machine.

11. Select the Re-spin function if, after processing, you want your processed treat softer and creamier.

12. Transfer the smoothie into serving bowls and serve immediately.

Chapter Sixty-Three

Cherry Berry Smoothie Bowl

Prep time: 10 minutes | Makes 2 servings

1 cup cranberry juice cocktail

¼ cup agave nectar

1 cup frozen cherry berry blend

1.

In a large bowl, add the agave nectar and cranberry juice cocktail and beat until well combined.

2. Place the cherry berry blend into an empty Ninja CREAMi pint container.

3. Top with cocktail mixture and stir to combine.

4. Cover the container with the storage lid and freeze for 24 hours.

5. After 24 hours, remove the lid from container and arrange into the outer bowl of Ninja CREAMi.

6. Install the "Creamerizer Paddle" onto the lid of outer bowl.

7. Then rotate the lid clockwise to lock.

8. Press "Power" button to turn on the unit.

9. Then press "SMOOTHIE BOWL" button.

10. When the program is completed, turn the outer bowl and release it from the machine.

11. Select the Re-spin function if, after processing, you want your processed treat softer and creamier.

12. Transfer the smoothie into serving bowls and serve immediately.

Chapter Sixty-Four

Mixed Berries Smoothie Bowl

Prep time: 10 minutes | Makes 4 servings

¾ cup fresh strawberries, hulled and quartered

¾ cup fresh raspberries

¾ cup fresh blueberries

¾ cup fresh blackberries

¼ cup plain Greek yogurt

1 tablespoon honey

1. In an empty Ninja CREAMi pint container, place the berries and with the back of a spoon, firmly press the berries below the MAX FILL line.

2. Add the yogurt and honey and stir to combine.

3. Cover the container with storage lid and freeze for 24 hours.

4. After 24 hours, remove the lid from container and arrange into the outer bowl of Ninja CREAMi.

5. Install the "Creamerizer Paddle" onto the lid of outer bowl.

6. Then rotate the lid clockwise to lock.

7. Press "Power" button to turn on the unit.

8. Then press "SMOOTHIE BOWL" button.

9. When the program is completed, turn the outer bowl and release it from the machine.

10. Select the Re-spin function if, after processing, you want your processed treat softer and creamier.

11. Transfer the smoothie into serving bowls and serve immediately.

Chapter Sixty-Five

Avocado Smoothie Bowl

Prep time: 10 minutes | Makes 4 servings

½ cup unsweetened coconut milk

¼ cup fresh apple juice

2 tablespoons whey protein isolate

4-5 tablespoons maple syrup

¼ teaspoon vanilla extract

1 cup ripe avocado, peeled, pitted and cut in ½-inch pieces

1 cup fresh banana, peeled and cut in ½-inch pieces

1. In a large bowl, add the coconut milk, apple juice, protein isolate, maple syrup and vanilla extract and beat until well combined.

2. Place the avocado and banana into an empty Ninja CREAMi pint container and with the back of a spoon, firmly press the fruit below the MAX FILL line.

3. Top with coconut milk mixture and mix until well combined.

4. Cover the container with the storage lid and freeze for 24 hours.

5. After 24 hours, remove the lid from container and arrange into the outer bowl of Ninja CREAMi.

6. Install the "Creamerizer Paddle" onto the lid of outer bowl.

7. Then rotate the lid clockwise to lock.

8. Press "Power" button to turn on the unit.

9. Then press "SMOOTHIE BOWL" button.

10. When the program is completed, turn the outer bowl and release it from the machine.

11. Select the Re-spin function if, after processing, you want your processed treat softer and creamier.

12. Transfer the smoothie into serving bowls and serve immediately.

Chapter Sixty-Six

Pumpkin Smoothie Bowl

Prep time: 10 minutes | Makes 2 servings

1 cup canned pumpkin puree

⅓ cup plain Greek yogurt

1½ tablespoons maple syrup

1 teaspoon vanilla extract

1 teaspoon pumpkin pie spice

1 frozen banana, peeled and cut in ½-inch pieces

Chapter Sixty-Seven

1. In an empty Ninja CREAMi pint container, add the pumpkin purée, yogurt, maple syrup, vanilla extract, and pumpkin pie spice and mix well.

2. Add the banana pieces and stir to combine.

3. Transfer the mixture into an empty Ninja CREAMi pint container.

4. Arrange the container into the outer bowl of Ninja CREAMi.

5.

Install the "Creamerizer Paddle" onto the lid of outer bowl.

6. Then rotate the lid clockwise to lock.

7. Press "Power" button to turn on the unit.

8. Then press "SMOOTHIE BOWL" button.

9. When the program is completed, turn the outer bowl and release it from the machine.

10. Select the Re-spin function if, after processing, you want your processed treat softer and creamier.

11. Transfer the smoothie into serving bowls and serve immediately.

The Mean Green Monster Smoothie

Prep time: 5 minutes | Cook time: 5 minutes|
Serves 2

½ cup baby spinach

½ apple peeled, cored, and chopped

½ banana, sliced

¼ cup carrots, chopped

½ cup fresh strawberries

¼ cup orange juice

½ cup ice

1. In an empty ninja CREAMi Pint, combine the spinach, apples, bananas, carrots, orange juice, strawberries, and ice.

2. In the outer bowl, place the Ninja CREAMi Pint. In the Ninja CREAMi machine, place the outer bowl with the Pint inside and

turn until the outer bowl locks into place. SMOOTHIE: Press the SMOOTHIE button. The ingredients will combine and become very creamy during the SMOOTHIE function.

3. Turn the outer bowl and remove it from the ninja CREAMi machine once the SMOOTHIE function has finished.

4. Select the Re-spin function if, after processing, you want your processed treat softer and creamier.

5. Fill a glass halfway with the smoothie.

Chapter Sixty-Eight

Strawberry Orange Crème Smoothie

Prep time: 5 minutes | Cook time: 5 minutes|
Serves 2

¼ cup orange juice

¼ cup ice cubes

½ cup fresh strawberries, hulled

1 container Greek Yogurt

10 ounces orange crème yogurt

1. Put all the ingredients into an empty ninja CREAMi Pint.

2. Place the Ninja CREAMi Pint into the outer bowl. Place the outer bowl with the Pint into the ninja CREAMi machine and turn until the outer bowl locks into place. Push the SMOOTHIE button. During the SMOOTHIE function, the ingredients will mix together and become very creamy.

3. Once the SMOOTHIE function has ended, turn the outer bowl and release it from the ninja CREAMi machine.

4. Select the Re-spin function if, after processing, you want your processed treat softer and creamier.

5. Scoop the smoothie into a tall glass.

Healthy Avocado Smoothie

Prep time: 5 minutes | Cook time: 5 minutes|
Serves 4

8 ice cubes

½ cup vanilla yogurt

1 ripe avocado, pitted

3 tablespoons honey

1 cup milk

1. Combine the avocado, milk, yogurt, honey, and ice cubes in an empty ninja CREA-
   Mi pint.

2. In the outer bowl, place the Ninja CREAMi
   pint. Insert the outer bowl containing the

pint into the Ninja CREAMi machine and turn until the outer bowl is locked into place. Select the smoothie option.

3. The ingredients will combine and become very creamy during the smoothie function.

4. Turn the outer bowl and remove it from the Ninja CREAMi device once the smoothie function has concluded.

5. Select the Re-spin function if, after processing, you want your processed treat softer and creamier.

6. Pour the smoothie into glasses.

Chapter Sixty-Nine

Choco Butter Banana Smoothie

Prep time: 5 minutes | Cook time: 5 minutes| Serves 2

2 cups chocolate pudding

1 cup ice cubes

1 cup whipped chocolate dairy topping

2 tablespoons of peanut butter

2 large ripe bananas

¾ cup milk

1. Puree the bananas in a large container and add all the other Ingredients except for the whipped topping. Combine and put into the ninja C REA Mi pint.

2. Place the pint into the outer container. Insert the outer bowl containing the pint into the Ninja CREAMi machine and turn until the outer bowl is locked into place. Select the smoothie option. The ingredients will combine to form a very creamy mixture.

3. Turn the outer bowl and remove it from the Ninja CREAMi machine once the smoothie function has finished.

4. Select the Re-spin function if, after processing, you want your processed treat softer and creamier.

5.

Scoop the smoothie into glass bowls to serve.

Dulce De Leche Milkshake

Prep time: 5 minutes | Cook time: 5 minutes| Serves 2

1 cup vanilla or coffee ice cream

½ cup milk

2 tablespoons sweetened condensed milk

¼ teaspoon salt

1. Place all Ingredients into an empty CREA-Mi Pint.

2. Place Pint in outer bowl, install Creamer-izer Paddle onto outer bowl lid and lock the lid assembly on the outer bowl. Place the bowl assembly on the motor base and crank the lever to elevate and secure the platform in place.

3. Choose the MILKSHAKE option.

4. Select the Re-spin function if, after processing, you want your processed treat softer and creamier.

5. Remove the milkshake from the Pint after the function is finished.

Choco-Hazelnut Milkshake

Prep time: 5 minutes | Cook time: 5 minutes| Serves 2

½ cup whole milk

¼ cup hazelnut spread

1 and ½ cup chocolate ice cream

1. Fill an empty CREAMI pint with ice cream.

2. Using a spoon, make a 1-inch wide hole in the bottom of the pint. Fill in the rest of the ingredients in the hole.

3. Fill the outer bowl with a pint, place the Creamerizer Paddle on the lid, and secure the lid assembly to the outer bowl. To raise and lock the platform in place, place the bowl assembly on the motor base and twist the handle to the right.

4. Choose the option for a milkshake.

5. Select the Re-spin function if, after processing, you want your processed treat softer and creamier.

6. Remove the milkshake from the pint and serve immediately after it has finished processing.

Cherry Chocolate Milkshake

Prep time: 5 minutes | Cook time: 5 minutes| Serves 2

1 and ½ cups chocolate ice cream

½ cup canned cherries, in syrup

¼ cup whole milk

1. Pour all ingredients in an empty CREAMI pint.

2. Put pint in outer bowl, install Creamerizer Paddle onto outer bowl lid, and lock the lid component on the outer bowl. Place the bowl component on the motor base and crank the lever to elevate and secure the platform in place.

3. Choose the milkshake option.

4. Select the Re-spin function if, after processing, you want your processed treat softer and creamier.

5. Remove the milkshake from the pint once the processing is done.

Chapter Seventy

Classic Cookie Milkshake

Prep time: 5 minutes | Cook time: 5 minutes| Serves 2

1 cup whole milk

1/2 cup amaretto-flavored coffee creamer

½ cup amaretto liqueur

1 tablespoon agave nectar

¼ cup chopped chocolate chip cookies

1. In a large mixing bowl, combine the milk, coffee creamer, amaretto liqueur, and agave nectar. Pour the mixture into a clean CREAMi Pint. Combine everything in a thorough mixing motion. Freeze the container for 24 hours while keeping the storage cover on it.

2. Take the Pint out of the freezer and remove the lid from the container. Placing the Pint in the outer bowl of your Ninja CREAMi and installing the Creamerizer Paddle in the outer bowl lid before locking the lid assembly to the outer bowl is recommended. To raise and secure the platform in place, place the bowl assembly on the motor base and twist the handle to the right until the platform is raised and secured.

3.

Select MILKSHAKE from the drop-down menu.

4. Select the Re-spin function if, after processing, you want your processed treat softer and creamier.

5. The cover should be removed once the machine has completed its processing. First, use a spoon to make a hole in the bottom of the Pint that is 1 2 inches wide. Next, replace the lid on the Pint and press the MIX-IN button. Finally, add the chopped cookies to the hole in the Pint.